How INEC Cripples The Giant of Africa

(Exposing the Rot in the Nigerian Electoral System)

P. O. Nwankwo, MCIArb

Contents

INTRODUCTION

Elections are the bedrock of any democracy, providing a legitimate mechanism through which citizens choose their leaders and influence governance. The strength of a democracy is often measured by the credibility of its electoral processes, as free, fair, and transparent elections ensure that the government derives its authority from the people. In Nigeria, a nation often referred to as the "Giant of Africa" due to its population, economic potential, and cultural influence, the importance of credible elections cannot be overstated. However, the reality of Nigeria's electoral system has frequently fallen short of this ideal, raising critical questions about the role of the Independent National Electoral Commission (INEC) in fulfilling its constitutional mandate.

INEC, established to manage and oversee elections in Nigeria, is central to the country's democratic process. It is tasked with ensuring that elections are conducted in a manner that upholds integrity, transparency, and the will of the people. However, in practice, INEC's performance has often been marred by allegations of corruption, inefficiency, partisanship, and a lack of accountability. These shortcomings have not only eroded public trust in the electoral process but have also hindered Nigeria's progress toward achieving a truly representative democracy.

This book, How INEC Cripples The Giant of Africa: Exposing the Rot in the Nigerian Electoral System, delves into the structural, operational, and ethical challenges facing INEC and their implications for Nigeria's democratic journey. It aims to provide a comprehensive analysis of the systemic issues that have plagued Nigeria's elections, from voter disenfranchisement and electoral fraud to the misuse of technology and logistical failures.

The objectives of this book are threefold:

1. **To highlight the critical role of credible elections in sustaining democracy and fostering good governance.**

2. **To scrutinize INEC's constitutional responsibilities and evaluate its performance in ensuring free and fair elections.**
3. **To propose actionable recommendations for reforming Nigeria's electoral system, thereby strengthening democracy and restoring public confidence in the process.**

Through detailed case studies, expert insights, and data-driven analysis, this book exposes the deep-seated issues that continue to undermine Nigeria's electoral integrity. It challenges stakeholders—government officials, civil society, political parties, and citizens—to demand and implement necessary reforms to safeguard the future of democracy in Africa's most populous nation.

The journey to fixing Nigeria's electoral system is not merely about holding INEC accountable; it is about reclaiming the promise of democracy and ensuring that the voices of the Nigerian people are genuinely heard and respected. The stakes could not be higher, for the health of Nigeria's democracy impacts not only its citizens but also the continent and the global community at large.

CHAPTER ONE

THE BIRTH OF INEC

Nigeria's journey toward democratic governance has been fraught with twists and turns, characterized by alternating periods of military rule and civilian administrations. Central to this struggle has been the quest to establish credible electoral processes—processes that reflect the will of the people. This chapter delves into the historical evolution of electoral commissions in Nigeria, the creation of the Independent National Electoral Commission (INEC), and its early successes and challenges.

Historical Evolution of Electoral Commissions in Nigeria

Nigeria's electoral journey began under colonial rule, with the 1922 Clifford Constitution introducing limited franchise elections in Lagos and Calabar. Although rudimentary, these elections planted the seeds for a system of electoral governance.

The post-independence period saw the establishment of more formal electoral bodies, each struggling to establish credibility and effectiveness.

1. **The Electoral Commission of Nigeria (ECN)**
    Established in 1959, the ECN was the first nationwide electoral body in Nigeria. Tasked with overseeing the 1959 general elections that ushered in Nigeria's independence in 1960, the ECN faced accusations of bias and manipulation, particularly in the favor of colonial interests.

2. **Federal Electoral Commission (FEDECO)**
    Following independence, FEDECO was established in 1964 to manage Nigeria's elections. It oversaw the tumultuous 1964 general elections and the subsequent 1979 elections, marking Nigeria's return to civilian rule. However, allegations of electoral malpractice and a lack of independence marred its operations, contributing to political instability and

the eventual collapse of the Second Republic in 1983.

3. **National Electoral Commission (NEC)** The NEC emerged during the military era in the late 1980s and early 1990s, managing the annulled June 12, 1993, presidential election widely regarded as one of Nigeria's fairest elections. This annulment, however, underscored the vulnerability of electoral bodies to executive interference, eroding public trust in the electoral process.

These iterations revealed persistent challenges: lack of independence, susceptibility to manipulation, and a failure to inspire confidence in the electorate. Against this backdrop, the Independent National Electoral Commission (INEC) was conceived.

The Establishment of INEC and Its Intended Purpose

In 1998, during General Abdulsalami Abubakar's transitional government, INEC was established to oversee Nigeria's return to democracy. Its mandate was clear: to conduct free, fair, and credible elections and restore confidence in the democratic process. INEC was designed to be independent of political influence, with legal and financial autonomy enshrined in the 1999 Constitution and the Electoral Act.

INEC's creation signified a renewed commitment to democratic governance. Unlike its predecessors, INEC was envisioned as a robust institution capable of withstanding external pressures and guaranteeing electoral integrity. Its responsibilities included:

- **Voter Registration:** Ensuring a comprehensive and accurate voters' register.
- **Election Conduct:** Organizing elections at the federal, state, and local levels.
- **Monitoring Political Parties:** Ensuring compliance with electoral laws and promoting internal party democracy.
- **Education and Advocacy:** Raising awareness about electoral rights and

processes to foster public participation.

With these ambitious goals, INEC began operations amidst high expectations from Nigerians and the international community.

Early Successes and Challenges

INEC's inaugural task was the 1999 general elections that marked Nigeria's transition from military rule to democracy. While the elections succeeded in returning the country to civilian governance, they were marred by logistical challenges, allegations of rigging, and widespread irregularities. These flaws exposed the enormity of INEC's task and the systemic issues within Nigeria's electoral framework.

Early Successes

1. **Facilitating Democratic Transition:** Despite criticisms, INEC played a pivotal role in ending decades of military rule, paving the way for Nigeria's Fourth Republic.

2. **Institutional Development:** INEC began establishing structures and processes to improve election management, including training electoral officers and developing operational guidelines.

Early Challenges

1. **Logistical Inefficiencies:** Poor planning, late arrival of election materials, and inadequate training of personnel undermined the credibility of early elections.
2. **Political Interference:** The autonomy of INEC was frequently tested, with political actors seeking to influence electoral outcomes.
3. **Public Distrust:** Many Nigerians remained skeptical of INEC's ability to deliver credible elections, given the legacy of past electoral bodies.

The birth of INEC symbolized hope for a nation eager to rebuild its democratic institutions. However, as the following chapters will reveal, this hope has often been overshadowed by the realities of systemic corruption, inefficiency, and political interference—issues that continue to cripple the giant of Africa.

CHAPTER TWO

ANATOMY OF ELECTORAL CORRUPTION IN NIGERIA

Electoral corruption is a pervasive problem in Nigeria's democratic process, and the Independent National Electoral Commission (INEC) has often been implicated, whether overtly or covertly, in this systemic issue. Understanding the anatomy of electoral corruption requires dissecting its definition, identifying its various forms, and exploring how it infiltrates INEC's operations, often fueled by money and political influence.

Definition and Forms of Electoral Corruption

Electoral corruption encompasses any manipulation of the electoral process to produce an unfair advantage for certain candidates, parties, or interest groups. It undermines the principles of transparency, accountability, and fairness essential to democratic governance. In Nigeria, this corruption takes numerous forms, including:

- **Vote Buying:** Offering money or material incentives to voters to secure their votes.
- **Voter Intimidation:** Coercing voters through threats or violence to sway election outcomes.
- **Ballot Stuffing:** Illegal insertion of additional ballot papers into the ballot box.
- **Electoral Violence:** Orchestrated disruptions, including attacks on polling units and personnel, to discredit or influence the results.
- **Manipulation of Results:** Altering election outcomes through tampering with electronic or manual vote counts.
- **Abuse of Electoral Logistics:** Delays or diversion of electoral materials to disenfranchise voters in strongholds of political opponents.

These acts of corruption do not occur in isolation but are often the result of a compromised electoral management body. INEC, as the custodian of Nigeria's elections, is both a gatekeeper and a potential enabler of these corrupt practices.

How Corruption Manifests in INEC's Operations

The rot within INEC is deeply ingrained and manifests at various levels of its operations, including:

1. **Pre-Election Activities:**
   - **Compromised Voter Registration:** Inflating or suppressing the voter register to favor specific regions or parties.
   - **Partisan Delimitation of Constituencies:** Gerrymandering electoral boundaries to ensure an unfair advantage for a political party.
   - **Selective Accreditation of Observers:** Allowing biased observers while sidelining credible organizations to influence the narrative of electoral fairness.
2. **Election Day Malpractices:**
   - **Deliberate Logistics Failures:** Late arrival or diversion of sensitive materials to

strongholds of opposition parties.

- **Collusion with Political Actors:** INEC officials may work with politicians to manipulate polling outcomes through ballot box stuffing, voter suppression, or falsified results.
- **Disregard for Technological Safeguards:** Manipulation of biometric devices or electronic transmission systems to alter outcomes.

3. **Post-Election Subversion:**
   - **Compromised Adjudication Processes:** Collusion between INEC officials and political actors during tribunal hearings to legitimize manipulated results.
   - **Delayed Release of Results:** Creating a window for undue influence or tampering with the outcome.

Role of Money and Political Influence in Compromising INEC's Integrity

At the heart of electoral corruption is the corrosive role of money and political power, which compromise INEC's independence and integrity. Key manifestations include:

1. **Bribery and Coercion of INEC Officials:**
    - Wealthy politicians and political parties often bribe INEC staff to influence their actions, from rigging elections to tampering with sensitive data.
    - High-ranking officials within INEC may be pressured or incentivized to favor powerful interests, eroding the institution's credibility.
2. **Political Patronage:**
    - The appointment process for INEC leadership is often steeped in political patronage, ensuring that those at the helm are loyal to ruling parties or influential politicians. This subservience compromises the commission's autonomy.
3. **Weaponization of State Resources:**

- The ruling class frequently deploys state funds and apparatus to compromise INEC's functions, either through logistical sabotage or outright coercion of its officials.
  - Security agencies, meant to safeguard elections, are sometimes used to enforce partisan agendas under INEC's watch.
4. **Funding Gaps and Reliance on Political Donors:**
  - Limited financial autonomy forces INEC to rely on external funding, which often comes with strings attached, exposing it to undue influence.

Electoral corruption in Nigeria is not merely a flaw in the system but a deliberate subversion of democracy, enabled by systemic weaknesses within INEC. From pre-election manipulations to post-election compromises, INEC's operations have been infiltrated by corrupt practices driven by money and political influence. Addressing this issue requires a comprehensive overhaul of INEC's structure, ensuring independence, accountability, and resistance to the influence of power and money in Nigerian politics. Only then can the electoral process truly reflect the will of the people and restore Nigeria's status as the Giant of Africa.

CHAPTER THREE

RIGGING, MANIPULATION, AND ELECTORAL FRAUD

Electoral fraud has been a persistent bane in Nigeria's quest for credible and transparent elections. Despite the promise of democratic governance, the integrity of the electoral process has often been undermined by rigging and manipulation. This chapter delves into notable case studies of rigged elections, examines the role of INEC officials in enabling fraud, and highlights the tactics commonly used to subvert the will of the people.

Case Studies of Rigged Elections in Nigeria

The history of elections in Nigeria is littered with allegations and evidence of rigging, casting doubt on the credibility of the process. Some elections stand out as glaring examples of manipulation:

1. **The 2003 General Elections**:
   Nigeria's 2003 elections, which marked

the return of Olusegun Obasanjo to power, were riddled with irregularities. Reports from election observers, including the European Union and local civil society organizations, documented widespread violence, intimidation of voters, and ballot box snatching. In some areas, results were declared for polling units where voting never occurred.

2. **Ekiti State Governorship Election, 2014**:
The Ekiti gubernatorial election highlighted the role of financial inducements in swaying voter choices. Dubbed "stomach infrastructure," the incumbent administration distributed food and cash to potential voters. Audio recordings later revealed collusion between INEC officials and political actors to manipulate the outcome in favor of the ruling party.

3. **Kogi State Governorship Election, 2019**:
This election was marred by violence and allegations of ballot stuffing. Observers reported incidents where

armed thugs disrupted polling units, disenfranchising voters. Despite the chaos, results were announced in favor of the incumbent, leading to protests and legal battles.

The Role of INEC Officials in Enabling Fraud

While external forces often orchestrate election rigging, the role of INEC officials cannot be overlooked. Compromised electoral officers have been implicated in various forms of malpractice, including:

- **Collusion with Politicians**:
  INEC officials are sometimes bribed or coerced into manipulating results at collation centers. This often involves falsifying figures or allowing unauthorized persons to gain access to sensitive materials.
- **Failure to Ensure Transparency**:
  Deliberate delays in the transmission of results create opportunities for tampering. The non-implementation of technological solutions, such as

electronic voting systems, has also been attributed to resistance from officials who benefit from manual processes prone to manipulation.
- **Sabotaging Electoral Processes**: Instances have emerged where INEC officials reportedly provided logistics information to political thugs, enabling disruptions at strategic polling units.

Tactics: Vote Buying, Ballot Stuffing, and Tampering with Results

Political actors employ a variety of tactics to rig elections, undermining the sanctity of the ballot. Below are the most common methods:

1. **Vote Buying**:
   The monetization of votes has become a hallmark of Nigerian elections. Political parties deploy agents who offer cash or gifts to voters in exchange for their votes. This practice not only corrupts the process but also perpetuates inequality, as wealthier parties hold an undue advantage.

2. **Ballot Stuffing**:
   A classic method of rigging, ballot stuffing involves adding extra votes to favor a particular candidate. This is often carried out in collusion with polling unit officials, who either turn a blind eye or actively participate in the act.
3. **Tampering with Results**:
   The manual collation process is particularly susceptible to tampering. Figures are inflated or altered during the journey from polling units to collation centers. In some cases, result sheets are replaced with falsified versions before reaching the final collation point.
4. **Intimidation and Violence**:
   Beyond logistical manipulation, the use of violence to scare away voters or opposition agents is a recurring tactic. This creates opportunities for fraudulent practices in areas where genuine voters have been displaced.
5. **Technological Manipulation**:
   As INEC increasingly adopts technology, such as the Biometric

Voter Accreditation System (BVAS) and electronic transmission of results, tech-savvy riggers have turned to hacking and other forms of digital interference to compromise these systems.

The Ripple Effect of Electoral Fraud

The consequences of rigging and electoral fraud extend beyond the immediate loss of a fair election. It erodes public trust in democratic institutions, perpetuates bad governance, and discourages citizen participation in future elections. The economic and social toll of fraudulent elections is immense, as leaders who emerge through rigging often prioritize personal gain over national development.

Electoral fraud, facilitated by rigging, manipulation, and systemic corruption, remains one of the greatest obstacles to Nigeria's democratic progress. While INEC bears significant responsibility for ensuring credible elections, the complicity of its officials and the elaborate schemes of political actors must be addressed. Only through stringent reforms, accountability measures, and active citizen engagement can Nigeria hope to restore the integrity of its electoral process and uphold the democratic ideals it strives to achieve.

CHAPTER FOUR

TECHNOLOGY AS A DOUBLE-EDGED SWORD

Introduction of Technology in the Electoral Process

In a bid to modernize and ensure transparency in Nigeria's electoral process, the Independent National Electoral Commission (INEC) embraced technology. The introduction of tools like the **Bimodal Voter Accreditation System (BVAS)** and the electronic transmission of results were heralded as a groundbreaking step towards free and fair elections. BVAS promised to eliminate issues like voter impersonation by accrediting voters through facial recognition and fingerprints, ensuring only legitimate voters cast their ballots. The electronic transmission of results aimed to curb manual collation malpractices by allowing real-time upload and viewing of results on INEC's result viewing portal.

These innovations generated widespread hope. For once, many Nigerians believed that technology could be the long-awaited antidote to the perennial electoral fraud that has plagued the country. Politicians, citizens, and international observers alike commended these developments, seeing them as a stride towards credibility. However, the excitement was short-lived, as the practical implementation of these technologies revealed significant flaws.

Challenges with Implementation and Misuse of Technology

While the deployment of electoral technology was promising, its implementation has been riddled with challenges, many of which reflect systemic inefficiencies within INEC. Key issues include:

1. **Inadequate Training and Deployment Failures:**
   INEC staff, especially ad hoc personnel, often receive insufficient training on operating these technologies. On election day, instances of BVAS

malfunctioning were rampant, ranging from failure to capture fingerprints to outright system crashes. This left voters disenfranchised and created opportunities for manipulation.

2. **Infrastructure Gaps:**
Nigeria's weak digital infrastructure—marked by unreliable internet connectivity, poor electricity supply, and inadequate backup systems—significantly hampers the seamless use of these technologies, especially in rural areas. In some cases, election officials resort to manual processes, defeating the purpose of technological advancements.

3. **Manipulation and Systematic Sabotage:**
The misuse of technology has also emerged as a major concern. BVAS devices have allegedly been tampered with to allow accreditation for non-existent voters, inflating voter turnout in certain regions. The electronic transmission of results, initially celebrated for its transparency, has faced frequent interruptions. Critics

argue that these "technical glitches" are deliberate, intended to provide room for tampering with results during manual collation.

4. **Lack of Accountability and Oversight:** Despite the promises of technology, INEC has been accused of failing to hold itself accountable for lapses. In instances where the BVAS failed or results were delayed, explanations were often vague, and investigations, if conducted, yielded no tangible consequences for those responsible.

Analysis of Cases Where Technology Was Used to Subvert the Electoral Process

Several high-profile elections in recent years illustrate how technology, while introduced to safeguard the process, has been weaponized to subvert the will of the people.

1. **2023 General Elections:** The 2023 elections were particularly controversial. BVAS devices were widely expected to ensure accuracy in voter accreditation and result

transmission. However, reports of deliberate non-activation of devices, coupled with the failure of INEC to upload results promptly, cast a shadow over the process. Observers pointed to regions where results were manually collated as hotspots for vote inflation and other manipulations.

2. **Off-Cycle Governorship Elections:** In some off-cycle elections, such as those in Edo and Anambra states, the electronic transmission system was cited as both a tool for transparency and a means of manipulation. While BVAS reduced incidents of overvoting in some areas, there were reports of its misuse to accredit unauthorized voters, particularly in strongholds of dominant political parties.

3. **Judicial Evidence from Election Tribunals:** Post-election tribunals have revealed the extent to which technology was exploited. In some cases, data from the BVAS devices contradicted figures declared by INEC. However, the commission's reluctance to provide

timely access to these devices and its failure to ensure a secure digital trail often leaves tribunals without enough evidence to overturn fraudulent results.

Technology is neither inherently good nor bad; it is a tool shaped by the systems and people who wield it. While innovations like BVAS and electronic result transmission have the potential to revolutionize Nigeria's elections, their misuse and the systemic rot within INEC threaten to turn these tools into weapons of disenfranchisement. Unless Nigeria addresses the underlying challenges of implementation, accountability, and transparency, technology will continue to serve as a double-edged sword in the country's quest for credible elections.

The promise of technology in elections is clear, but so too is the peril when such tools are deployed in a broken system. For Nigeria to rise as the true giant of Africa, INEC must evolve beyond superficial reforms and embrace a culture of integrity and accountability in its technological applications.

CHAPTER FIVE

EXTERNAL FORCES AND THE POLITICIZATION OF INEC

The Independent National Electoral Commission (INEC) was envisioned as the cornerstone of Nigeria's democracy, tasked with ensuring free, fair, and credible elections. However, its ability to fulfill this mandate has often been undermined by external forces that manipulate its processes for personal or partisan gain. This chapter delves into the external forces that have politicized INEC, with a particular focus on political interference, the role of security agencies, and the dichotomy between INEC's perceived impartiality and the realities on the ground.

Political Interference and Undue Influence from Power Brokers

Political interference remains one of the most significant threats to the independence of INEC. Power brokers—comprising political godfathers, ruling parties, and influential individuals—wield enormous influence over the electoral body. Through covert manipulation and overt intimidation, these actors often seek to tilt the scales in favor of their preferred candidates or parties.

This interference manifests in various ways, such as:

1. **Candidate Imposition:** Political elites pressure INEC to disqualify certain candidates under questionable pretexts, thereby limiting voters' choices.
2. **Manipulation of Electoral Timelines:** Delays in election scheduling or sudden shifts in dates are often linked to strategic calculations by powerful stakeholders aiming to destabilize opponents.
3. **Budgetary Dependence:** Despite constitutional provisions granting INEC financial autonomy, delays or withholding of funding by the executive arm create a dependency

that compromises the commission's independence.

These actions erode public trust in INEC's ability to conduct impartial elections, reinforcing perceptions of a compromised system.

The Role of Security Agencies in Enabling or Combating Electoral Fraud

The involvement of security agencies in elections is a double-edged sword. While their mandate includes maintaining law and order, their actions sometimes stray into the realm of enabling electoral fraud. In Nigeria, the military, police, and other security operatives have been accused of partisanship and complicity in electoral malpractices.

1. **Collusion with Political Actors:** Instances of security personnel providing cover for ballot box snatching, voter intimidation, and suppression are well-documented. These actions often occur in opposition strongholds or areas with high voter

turnout likely to threaten the ruling party.

2. **Selective Enforcement of Electoral Laws:** Security agencies are often accused of turning a blind eye to the activities of thugs employed by powerful politicians while clamping down heavily on opposition supporters.

3. **Positive Interventions:** Despite these challenges, there have been cases where security agencies played pivotal roles in preventing violence and apprehending perpetrators of electoral misconduct. However, such successes are sporadic and insufficient to counterbalance their overall role in undermining the system.

To ensure the integrity of elections, security agencies must be insulated from political pressures and held accountable for their actions.

INEC's Perceived Impartiality: Myths and Realities

INEC's claim of impartiality is a contentious topic in Nigeria. While the commission often asserts its commitment to neutrality, public perception suggests otherwise. This perceived lack of impartiality stems from systemic issues and anecdotal evidence of favoritism.

1. **Partisan Appointments:** The appointment of INEC officials, particularly the chairman, by the president has led to accusations of bias, especially when the appointing authority is an interested party in the election.
2. **Transparency Deficits:** The opaque nature of some INEC operations—such as the collation and announcement of results—fuels skepticism about its neutrality.
3. **Selective Accountability:** While INEC has penalized smaller parties and independent candidates for infractions, major parties and their candidates often escape with little or no repercussions for similar or worse offenses.

The politicization of INEC by external forces is a grave impediment to Nigeria's democratic progress. Political interference, compromised security agencies, and perceptions of bias have entrenched a culture of distrust and disillusionment among Nigerians. To restore faith in the electoral process, systemic reforms are imperative. These include granting INEC genuine autonomy, depoliticizing security agencies, and instituting measures to enhance transparency and accountability. Only then can Nigeria begin to realize the democratic ideals it so desperately seeks.

CHAPTER SIX

THE IMPACT ON DEMOCRACY AND NATIONAL DEVELOPMENT

The electoral process is the bedrock of democracy, shaping the legitimacy of governance and the development trajectory of any nation. In Nigeria, the Independent National Electoral Commission (INEC) is saddled with the monumental responsibility of organizing free, fair, and credible elections. However, the systemic flaws within INEC have far-reaching consequences, threatening democracy, eroding public trust, and crippling national development.

Weakened Governance and Institutional Trust

Flawed elections do not merely distort the democratic process; they undermine governance itself. Leaders who ascend to power through electoral fraud are often beholden to special interests rather than the electorate, leading to poor decision-making and governance that prioritizes personal or partisan gain over national interest.

This erosion of legitimacy breeds disillusionment among citizens, who view political office holders as undeserving or incapable of delivering on their mandates. Trust in public institutions such as the judiciary, law enforcement, and electoral bodies becomes collateral damage, creating a vicious cycle of mistrust and disengagement. In such an environment, institutions struggle to maintain authority, and the rule of law becomes tenuous, allowing corruption and impunity to flourish unchecked.

Electoral Corruption and Socioeconomic Development

The socioeconomic consequences of electoral corruption are profound. Elections marred by vote-buying, ballot-stuffing, and collusion between politicians and INEC officials divert resources away from critical sectors. Funds earmarked for education, healthcare, infrastructure, and job creation are often redirected to finance electoral malpractice or reward loyalists.

This misallocation perpetuates poverty, unemployment, and inequality, trapping Nigeria in a cycle of underdevelopment. Moreover, leaders who rise through corrupt electoral processes lack the incentive to prioritize long-term policies or structural reforms, focusing instead on short-term gains to secure their political survival. The ripple effect is a stagnant economy, brain drain, and weakened global standing, as Nigeria's potential remains largely untapped due to poor leadership.

Public Perception of INEC and Voter Apathy

Public perception of INEC is another critical factor in the erosion of democracy in Nigeria. Repeated allegations of electoral fraud, inefficiency, and partiality have tarnished the commission's image. Many Nigerians view INEC as complicit in the political elite's agenda, rather than as a neutral arbiter of democracy.

This perception fuels voter apathy, as citizens increasingly believe that their votes do not count. The decline in voter turnout in successive elections is a testament to the growing disenchantment with the electoral process. When the electorate feels disempowered, democratic participation wanes, further emboldening corrupt politicians and weakening the democratic fabric of the nation.

The Road Ahead

Addressing these challenges requires a comprehensive overhaul of Nigeria's electoral system. Strengthening INEC's independence, enforcing accountability measures, and leveraging technology to eliminate electoral malpractice are critical steps. Equally important is a robust campaign to restore public confidence in the electoral process, emphasizing the power and importance of individual votes in shaping Nigeria's future.

Until these issues are resolved, the rot in Nigeria's electoral system will continue to undermine democracy and national development, leaving the "Giant of Africa" perpetually hobbled by its own systemic failures.

CHAPTER SEVEN

VOICES OF THE MARGINALIZED

The Nigerian electoral system has long been a battleground for political power, but for many citizens, it is also a story of exclusion, frustration, and despair. The voices of women, youth, and minority groups—those who often find themselves at the margins of political discourse—reveal the deep cracks within the system. Their experiences highlight the cost of electoral malpractice and the urgent need for reform.

Stories of Disenfranchised Voters

The tale of Amina Bello, a widowed mother of three from northern Nigeria, exemplifies the plight of disenfranchised women. Amina stood in line for hours under the scorching sun, clutching her voter card and the hope of a brighter future. However, when the time came to vote, officials informed her that her polling unit had been relocated without prior notice. "It felt like my voice was stolen,"

Amina recounts. "How can I trust a system that treats me as invisible?"

Youth, who make up a significant portion of Nigeria's population, are similarly disillusioned. Take the case of Emeka Okoye, a first-time voter from Lagos. Despite registering and participating in the electoral process, Emeka discovered on election day that his name was inexplicably missing from the voter roll. His frustration mirrors the experiences of thousands who are eager to contribute to nation-building but are systematically shut out.

Minority groups face even greater challenges. In parts of the Niger Delta, for example, communities are deliberately excluded due to political calculations. These areas, often impoverished and riddled with infrastructural decay, are home to voters like Chief Ekanem, who describes his experience as "a calculated silencing of our people." Ballot boxes are destroyed, polling units are under-policed, and election results are manipulated, leaving entire communities disenfranchised.

The Cost of Failed Electoral Promises

The price of electoral promises that never materialize is paid by ordinary citizens. For Amina, the free healthcare program promised by the ruling party never reached her village. For Emeka, the pledged educational reforms that could have eased his burden as a student remain a mirage. For Chief Ekanem's community, promises of clean water and basic amenities remain unfulfilled as corrupt officials pocket development funds.

These broken promises erode trust in governance and deepen the cycles of poverty and despair. Disillusioned voters, once hopeful for change, find themselves grappling with the harsh realities of unfulfilled dreams. For the marginalized, elections are not a pathway to empowerment but a cruel charade that perpetuates their suffering.

The Role of Civil Society and Grassroots Movements

Amidst these challenges, civil society organizations and grassroots movements have emerged as critical actors in holding the Independent National Electoral Commission (INEC) accountable. Groups like the Nigeria Youth Movement for Transparency and Women for Electoral Justice are amplifying the voices of the marginalized, demanding systemic reforms, and championing the fight against voter suppression.

One inspiring example is the Coalition for Free and Fair Elections (CoFFE), which has mobilized communities across the country to report electoral malpractice. Through social media campaigns, town hall meetings, and legal advocacy, CoFFE has exposed several instances of voter suppression, ballot stuffing, and electoral violence. Their efforts have forced INEC to revisit questionable practices and implement some reforms, albeit reluctantly.

Grassroots movements like The Vote is My Voice initiative have empowered citizens to understand their rights and challenge systemic oppression. In marginalized communities, these movements provide training on how to report electoral fraud, ensure transparency at polling units, and demand accountability from public officials.

A Call to Action

The voices of the marginalized are a stark reminder that Nigeria's democracy remains fragile. Women, youth, and minority groups deserve more than tokenistic inclusion—they deserve a system that values their contributions and safeguards their rights. For this to happen, INEC must address its failings with urgency and sincerity.

The future of Nigeria's democracy depends on whether the cries of disenfranchised voters will transform into a chorus of empowered voices. This transformation will require not just institutional reforms but also the active participation of civil society, grassroots movements, and every Nigerian committed to justice and equity.

As we look ahead, the question remains: Will INEC rise to the challenge and become a beacon of democratic integrity, or will it continue to cripple the giant of Africa? The answer lies not just in the corridors of power but in the courage of the marginalized to demand the Nigeria they deserve.

CHAPTER EIGHT

REFORM OR REVOLUTION? THE WAY FORWARD

Nigeria's journey to establishing a robust and credible electoral process is one riddled with challenges, from systemic corruption to operational inefficiencies. The Independent National Electoral Commission (INEC), as the cornerstone of Nigeria's electoral process, must undergo significant transformation to fulfill its mandate effectively. This chapter explores critical areas requiring urgent reform, presents recommendations for legislative and institutional changes, and highlights the roles of technology, civil society, and international observers in fostering credible elections.

Key Areas Requiring Urgent Reform

1. Funding

The funding of INEC has long been a source of controversy. Inconsistent budget allocations and undue political interference have hampered its ability to operate independently. A transparent, predictable, and constitutionally guaranteed funding mechanism is crucial to reduce susceptibility to manipulation by political actors.

Key Recommendations:

- **Legislative Safeguards**: Enact laws mandating the direct disbursement of funds to INEC as part of the consolidated revenue fund to eliminate delays and undue influence.
- **Financial Transparency**: INEC must publish detailed financial reports outlining how funds are allocated and spent to build public trust.
- **External Oversight**: Establish an independent audit body to scrutinize INEC's financial operations regularly.

2. Personnel

INEC's personnel, from top officials to ad hoc staff, often face accusations of partiality, incompetence, or outright collusion with political actors. Strengthening the integrity and professionalism of its workforce is non-negotiable for electoral credibility.

Key Recommendations:

- **Comprehensive Training**: Develop rigorous training programs emphasizing ethics, technical competence, and impartiality for both permanent and ad hoc staff.
- **Recruitment Standards**: Institute merit-based recruitment processes to ensure only qualified and committed individuals are employed.
- **Accountability Mechanisms**: Implement a zero-tolerance policy for electoral malpractice, with severe penalties for personnel found guilty of misconduct.

3. Accountability Mechanisms

The lack of accountability within INEC has emboldened malpractice and eroded public confidence in the electoral process.

Key Recommendations:

- **Whistleblower Protections**: Establish secure channels for whistleblowers to report malpractice without fear of reprisal.
- **Independent Review Panels**: Set up independent electoral review panels to investigate allegations of misconduct during and after elections.
- **Performance Evaluation**: Institute a performance monitoring system to evaluate the effectiveness of INEC's operations, with actionable insights for continuous improvement.

Recommendations for Legislative and Institutional Changes

1. Electoral Act Revisions

The Electoral Act must be continually updated to address emerging challenges and close loopholes. Priority areas include:

- **Strengthening Penalties**: Introduce stiffer penalties for electoral offences, including vote-buying, tampering with results, and voter intimidation.

- **Electronic Voting**: Fully integrate electronic voting and result transmission to minimize human interference and errors.
- **Autonomy Provisions**: Enhance INEC's independence by insulating it from political interference through explicit constitutional protections.

2. Judicial Reforms

The judiciary plays a pivotal role in resolving electoral disputes. However, delays and inconsistencies undermine the process.

- **Special Electoral Tribunals**: Establish fast-track electoral tribunals with strict timelines for adjudicating disputes.
- **Judicial Oversight**: Implement mechanisms to prevent corruption and ensure impartiality in the handling of electoral cases.

3. Collaboration with Other Institutions

INEC cannot work in isolation. Its success depends on effective collaboration with security agencies, anti-corruption bodies, and civic institutions.

- **Security Protocols**: Develop comprehensive election security plans in partnership with the police and other security agencies to safeguard voters and election materials.
- **Partnership with Anti-Corruption Agencies**: Work closely with bodies like the Economic and Financial Crimes Commission (EFCC) to investigate and prosecute electoral offenders.

The Role of Technology, Civil Society, and International Observers

1. Leveraging Technology

Technology offers a pathway to transparency and efficiency in elections.

- **Electronic Voting Systems**: Expand the deployment of electronic voting systems, ensuring they are reliable, user-friendly, and accessible.

- **Blockchain for Results Transmission**: Utilize blockchain technology to securely transmit and verify election results.
- **Biometric Verification**: Strengthen the use of biometric verification to eliminate voter impersonation and other forms of fraud.

2. Civil Society Organizations (CSOs)

CSOs are essential in holding INEC accountable and ensuring public participation.

- **Voter Education**: Partner with CSOs to educate citizens about their rights and responsibilities during elections.
- **Monitoring and Reporting**: Support CSOs in deploying independent election monitors to observe and report irregularities.
- **Advocacy**: Collaborate with CSOs to push for necessary electoral reforms through public campaigns and policy dialogues.

3. International Observers

The presence of international observers can enhance credibility and deter malpractices.

- **Capacity Building**: Engage international partners to train INEC officials and electoral observers.
- **Observation Missions**: Encourage reputable international organizations to observe elections and publish unbiased reports.
- **Global Benchmarks**: Leverage global best practices to improve Nigeria's electoral process.

Reform, not revolution, is the sustainable path forward for INEC and Nigeria's electoral system. While the challenges are profound, the solutions are within reach, provided there is political will and collective action. By addressing the critical issues of funding, personnel integrity, and accountability mechanisms, supported by legislative changes and the strategic deployment of technology, Nigeria can build a credible and transparent electoral process. Civil society and international actors must also play their part, fostering vigilance and innovation to ensure the Giant of Africa can truly stand tall on the global stage.

CONCLUSION

Nigeria's status as the "Giant of Africa" is a testament to its vast potential, rich cultural heritage, and abundant human and natural resources. Yet, as revealed in this book, the persistent failures of the Independent National Electoral Commission (INEC) threaten to undermine that identity. Our findings expose systemic flaws in Nigeria's electoral system, from logistical inefficiencies and lack of transparency to blatant instances of corruption and manipulation. These issues not only erode public trust but also perpetuate a cycle of poor governance, leaving millions of Nigerians disillusioned and disenfranchised.

The urgent need for reform cannot be overstated. INEC must undergo a comprehensive overhaul to become a truly independent and transparent institution. This requires the enforcement of stricter accountability mechanisms, the adoption of cutting-edge technology to minimize human interference, and the establishment of robust safeguards against electoral malpractice. Beyond INEC, reforms must address the broader political culture that tolerates and even rewards such failures.

This is a clarion call to all Nigerians: citizens, policymakers, and global stakeholders alike. Citizens must rise above apathy and demand accountability from those entrusted with safeguarding democracy. Civil society organizations, legal practitioners, and the media must amplify their advocacy for electoral reforms and hold INEC accountable. Policymakers must prioritize legislation that strengthens electoral integrity and eliminates loopholes for exploitation. International partners and observers must sustain their interest in Nigeria's democratic process, offering both technical support and diplomatic pressure to ensure credible elections.

The vision for a transparent and credible electoral system in Nigeria is not an unattainable dream. Imagine a nation where every vote truly counts, where leaders emerge based on merit rather than manipulation, and where elections become a source of unity rather than division. This vision is achievable, but it requires collective will, unyielding determination, and unwavering commitment to democratic principles.

Nigeria's future depends on the integrity of its electoral process. It is time for every stakeholder to take a stand. Together, we can dismantle the rot within INEC and rebuild a system that upholds the values of fairness, justice, and equity. Only then can Nigeria reclaim its rightful place as a true giant of Africa, leading by example in the pursuit of democracy, accountability, and progress.

Appendix A: Timeline of Major Controversies in Nigerian Elections

This timeline highlights significant controversies that have shaped Nigeria's electoral landscape, emphasizing their impact on democratic development and governance.

- **1964-1965 General Elections**
  - Allegations of widespread rigging, voter suppression, and political violence.
  - Culminated in the Western Region Crisis, contributing to Nigeria's first military coup in 1966.
- **1979 General Election**
  - Dispute over the interpretation of the "12 2/3 states" requirement for presidential victory.
  - Supreme Court's ruling favored Shehu Shagari, raising questions about judicial impartiality.
- **1993 Presidential Election**

- o Widely regarded as Nigeria's freest and fairest election, won by Moshood Abiola.
  - o Annulled by the military government, sparking nationwide protests and political instability.
- **2007 General Elections**
  - o Described by international observers as one of Nigeria's worst elections due to ballot stuffing, violence, and lack of transparency.
- **2015 General Elections**
  - o First election where an incumbent president, Goodluck Jonathan, conceded defeat.
  - o Marked by significant improvements in technology use (introduction of PVCs and card readers) but marred by logistics challenges.
- **2023 General Elections**
  - o Use of BVAS and IReV technology faced implementation challenges, leading to widespread

allegations of result manipulation and electoral fraud.

Appendix B: Relevant Laws Governing INEC and Elections in Nigeria

This section provides a summary of key legal frameworks that guide INEC's operations and elections in Nigeria.

1. **Constitution of the Federal Republic of Nigeria, 1999 (as amended)**
    - **Section 153**: Establishes INEC as an independent body.
    - **Third Schedule, Part 1, Item F**: Details INEC's powers, functions, and composition.
2. **Electoral Act, 2022**
    - **Section 47**: Mandates electronic transmission of results.
    - **Section 50(2)**: Authorizes the use of technology in the electoral process.
    - **Section 64**: Governs the collation and announcement of results.

3. **INEC Guidelines and Regulations**
    - Issued periodically to provide operational details on voter registration, accreditation, and result management.
4. **Political Parties Act**
    - Regulates party registration, funding, and conduct during elections.

Appendix C: Comparative Analysis of Electoral Commissions in Africa

This appendix compares the Independent National Electoral Commission (INEC) with other prominent electoral bodies across Africa, focusing on structure, independence, and performance.

Country	Electoral Commission	Key Features	Challenges
Nigeria	Independent National Electoral Commission (INEC)	Constitutional body; oversees all electoral processes; employs	Logistics issues, political interference, funding

Country	Electoral Commission	Key Features	Challenges
South Africa	Electoral Commission of South Africa (IEC)	technology such as BVAS and IReV. Highly autonomous; robust voter education programs; excellent logistics management.	constraints. Allegations of slow adaptation to technology.
Ghana	Electoral Commission of Ghana	Transparent election processes; proactive stakeholder engagement; efficient technology integration.	Limited resources for large-scale elections.
Kenya	Independent Electoral and	Advanced use of technology (e.g., KIEMS kits); clear	Frequent court cases challenging

Country	Electoral Commission	Key Features	Challenges
	Boundaries Commission (IEBC)	legal framework for dispute resolution.	results.
Senegal	Autonomous National Electoral Commission (CENA)	Decentralized structure; emphasizes inclusivity through diaspora voting.	Occasional issues with voter registration.

These appendices provide essential context for understanding the challenges and opportunities within Nigeria's electoral system, encouraging informed discussions about reforms.